Wíyouŋkihipi Productions: Dakhóta owned-and-operating on the traditional homelands of the Dakhóta Oyáte.
Imníža Ská Othúŋwe, Mnísota / Saint Paul, Minnesota

For more information on this book including audio guides, visit www.wiyounkihipi.com

Designed by Marlena Myles
Main body text set in Change Serif
Typeface provided from Mateusz Machalski

Library of Congress Cataloging-in-Publication Data
The Cataloging-in-Publication Data for Prairie Bones is on file at the Library of Congress
ISBN 978-1-956981-04-9 (print lib. bdg. edition here)
ISBN 978-1-956981-05-6 (ebook edition here)

Printed in the United States of America

This work is funded in part by the Minnesota Humanities Center with money from the Arts and Cultural Heritage Fund that was created with the vote of the people of Minnesota on November 4, 2008. Wóphida tháŋka!

PRAIRIE BONES

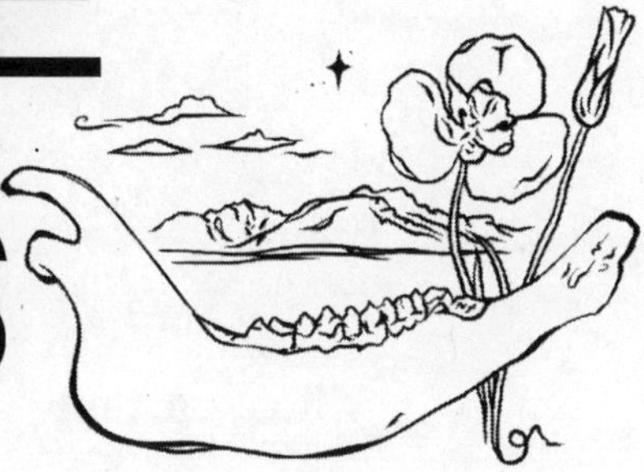

a collection of poems about reconnecting with Lakȯta kin, culture, and learning what it means to stand alongside all the relatives of this land to fight for liberation

ROBERT HAROLD BORDEAUX

WITH ILLUSTRATIONS BY
THOMASINA TOPBEAR

Wíyouŋkihipi Productions
Imníža Ská Othúŋwe, Mnísota • (Saint Paul, Minnesota)

The definition of 'reconnect' states
that it is the re-establishing of a bond or emotion.
The word alone points toward a story of separation. As a reconnecting Lak̇ot̄a, it is known that this story of separation speaks of the years of
colonial violence brought by colonizers
who came to this land in not a good way.

I exist, as many of us do,
with many complexities deep in my bones. Both Lak̇ot̄a and colonizer ancestry flows through my veins. This does not mean, however, that I'm not fully Lak̇ot̄a. I'm learning that being Lak̇ot̄a means carrying on teachings, knowledge, and culture to my children and their children
and their children (and so on). It means being a good relative.
It means existing as a contradiction to the colonial systems that tried
to erase my Lak̇ot̄a ancestors (to no avail).

I share these words to share a piece of my story. To share a piece of what I'm learning. And to slowly reclaim space for my people in a good way. I offer these words to you as a testament to the strength of my ancestors from seven generations ago who prayed for my breath and the ensuing generations who carried on those prayers while
adding to them with their prayers for
the generations to come.

Colonial violence in the form of genocide and assimilation nearly put the Lak̇ot̄a language to sleep. Resistance to this violence by Lak̇ot̄a kin who put their lives on the line to keep the language alive is the reason why the language is still awake. My family holds stories of being beaten for speaking it in the boarding school they attended. Many lost their lives fighting to preserve Lak̇ot̄a language and culture. Lak̇ot̄a spirituality and ceremonies were illegal to practice in the United States until 1978. I ask of you to consider these stories and remember the sacrifices Lak̇ot̄a kin made so that your eyes may share space with these Lak̇ot̄a words and phrases in this moment.

Lila wopila to Albert White Hat, Sr. (and all others involved) in creating the Lak̇ot̄a Iyap̄i writing system used in this book.

**Glossary for the Lak̇ot̄a language usage in this text is located in the back of this book.*

CONTENTS

2.

NAĠI (soul) 31

3.

UŊČI MAKȞA (grandmother earth) 55

4.

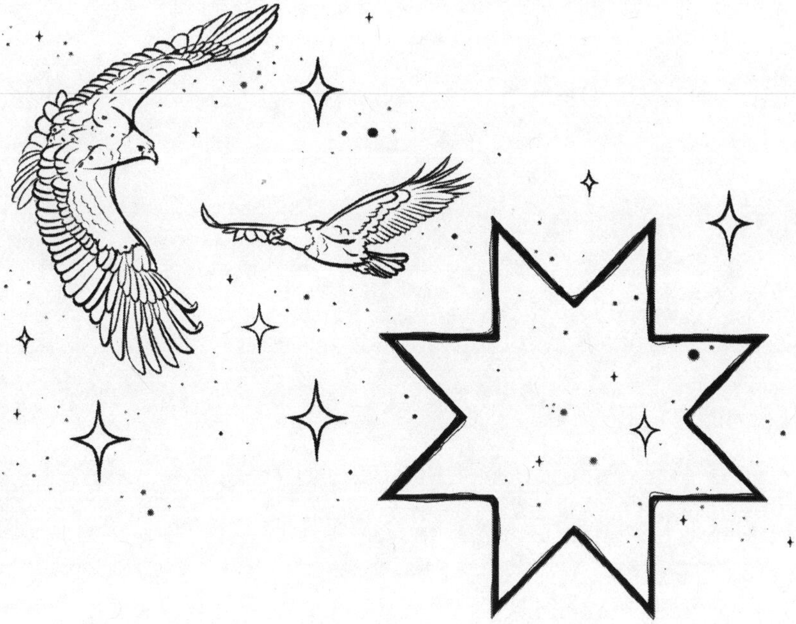

1.

WIĊAHUŊK̄AK̄E

(ancestors)

BEGINNINGS

I come from the dirt,
the seed of a wildflower
that found itself
in the ditch of a South Dakota country road.

I come from the soil,
the tomato plant
in my grandparents' garden
cared for and raised by their hands.

I come from the mud,
a swirl of many things
maka mixed with *mni*
mixed with the roots of all our plant relatives.

I come from *Uŋčī Maka*,
in the form of prayers from *wičahuŋkake*
as they guide me to every fragment I lost at birth
and teach me what it means to be
whole.

EMBRACING THE SUN

I remember wearing sweaters
in the middle of summer
to hide from the sunlight.

The complexity of my *wiċahuŋk̄ak̄e* revealed
as the sun kissed my body.
Light-skinned,
mixed,
a swirl of clashing worlds
whose fragments got stitched together
into me.

So I would hide in the shadows,
full of sweat in long-sleeves
playing outside when it was 100 degrees,
because if I could blend in
I could avoid the jabs and blows
from those who would let me know
I don't fit in.

Growing up,
I was taught
that the sun is a star,
but I wasn't taught
how we descend from,
are guided by
wiċaḣp̄e

And now I know why
I've always felt the stardust
deep in my bones.

All along,
the stars have been validating my existence,
patiently waiting for me to see
every piece of who I am.

Every complexity,
every fragment,
stitched together
perfectly
into me.

THE LOST ART OF LISTENING TO YOUR HEART

I feel the *ṫataŋk̄a* in my veins
with every heartbeat.

Their hooves pound in rhythm with my pulse.

I follow them to a familiar place
yet, unknown to me.

I think I'll stay awhile.

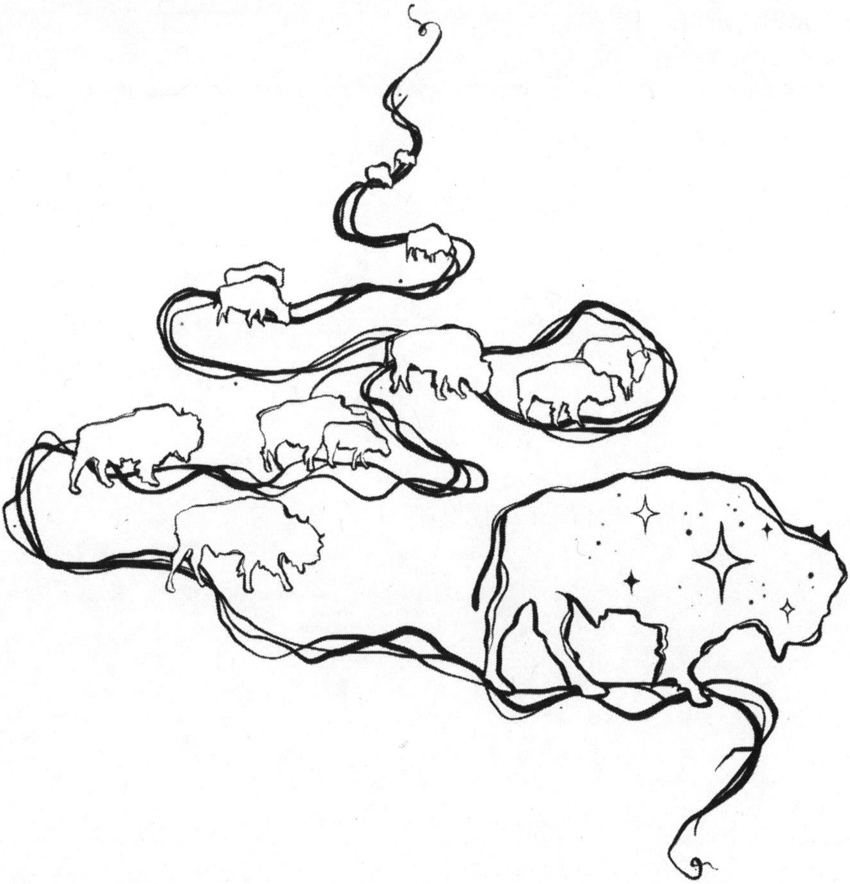

UNDERNEATH MY RIBS

parts of me feel / fragmented / books / speak of / mix-bloods /
speak of a people / fragmented / but my *wiċahuŋk̄ak̄e* / aren't fragments /
they teach me / underneath my ribs / I am / simply / Lak̇ot̄a

GENERATIONAL HEALING

In my heart,
it is from disconnect
caused by colonial violence
that weeds grow
and strangle
the roots of healing.

It is my hands
guided by *wićahuŋk̄ak̄e*
that allows me to
tend to this garden
to build a foundation of soil
where mending can grow.

DREAMS

Wiċahuŋk̄ak̄e visit me
in my dreams.
They guide me,
they protect me,
they show me their prayers
from generations ago
and I see how my breath
looks like the words
they prayed.

PERSEVERANCE

I'd like to think
there is enough left of me
to live courageously
after I shatter and rebuild,
shatter and rebuild,
shatter and rebuild.

Rebuild on the foundation
those who came before laid with resilience.

Rebuild for those who will breathe life
seven generations from now.

ME, REWRITTEN

I've let go of the story written for myself
through the lens of colonialism
and now my pen runs free,
the ink bleeding on every inch of the paper.
A ledger art masterpiece.
A swirl of color.
A swirl of reclamation.

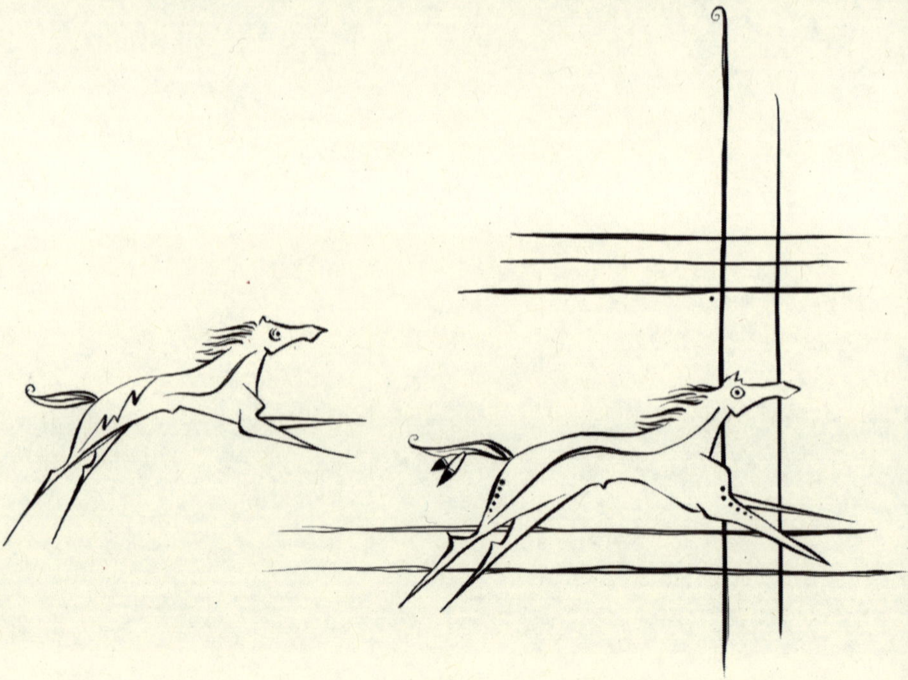

HOMECOMING

I found myself on a backroad
toward *Mniluzahaŋ*
while *wí* was setting.

Ḣe Sap̄a greeted me
with a sunset fire
over the hills.

I've tasted four decades.
Seen life and death
all around and within myself
but still,
I feel like a *hokśič̄ala*,
so young
still growing
in the Laḱot̄a way.

Every time I find my way here
it feels like the first time,
always listening
always learning
from *wičahuŋḱak̄e*.

As I settled in to find rest in *Ḣe Sap̄a*
among the trees,
the *wak̄iŋyaŋ* welcomed me home.

And as they sang their songs,
I dance to them
freely in the rain.

Broken treaties will never
break my spirit.
This land will always be
my home.

THOSE WHO CAME BEFORE

I step into the grass
and let my toes meet the blades
in a dance.

I close my eyes
and feel those who came before
swim in my veins
all the way to my heart
as I learn from
these stewards of the land
my feet rest on
and the knowledge they hold.

I exhale softly
and breath in hope
as I learn what it means
to carry on this fight
for healing and justice
for *Uŋċi Maka.*

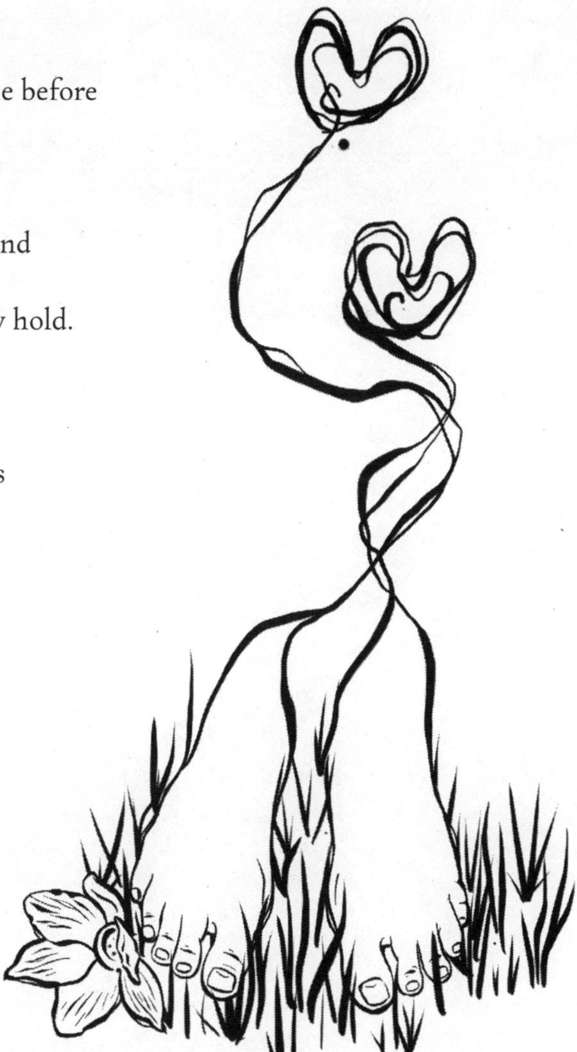

AK̄IĊIT̄A

The same air
that filled the lungs
of those who came before
now fills your lungs,
so hold steadfast
to the ak̄iċit̄a
that flows
through your veins.

Let their strength
pump from your heart
to every part of you
and let your body
remember
what it means
to descend from
wiċaḣp̄i.

BRIDGE (NOUN)

- something that is intended to
reconcile or form a connection between two things.

If those two things are the wisdom of those who came before
and future generations, disrupted by colonization
then let my hands be a bridge.
Let my heart be a bridge.
Let my voice be a bridge.
Let my life be a bridge.

I pray to be a bridge for what was
and what will always be
a living, breathing people.

MY ANCESTORS' TONGUE (IN THREE PARTS)

PT. 1
My bones ache.

They know of a time
before the disease
brought here by boats.

They know of a time
before the quiet cries
of this hurting earth,
both soil and water
sick from exploitation.

They know of a time
before a culture severed,
red spilled between
the beauty of what was
and assimilation.

My *wičahuŋk̄ak̄e* sing
and my bones ache
because I do not know their words.

PT. 2

I saw an eagle fly over I-70.
I whispered to myself *waŋblí*.
There is so much I do not yet know,
but with every word I learn in Lak̇ōta,
I think about what it will sound like
hearing my children say them back to me.
I think about how my ancestors will get to hear
the future generation's children they prayed for
speak in their tongue.
And that alone carries me toward every tomorrow.

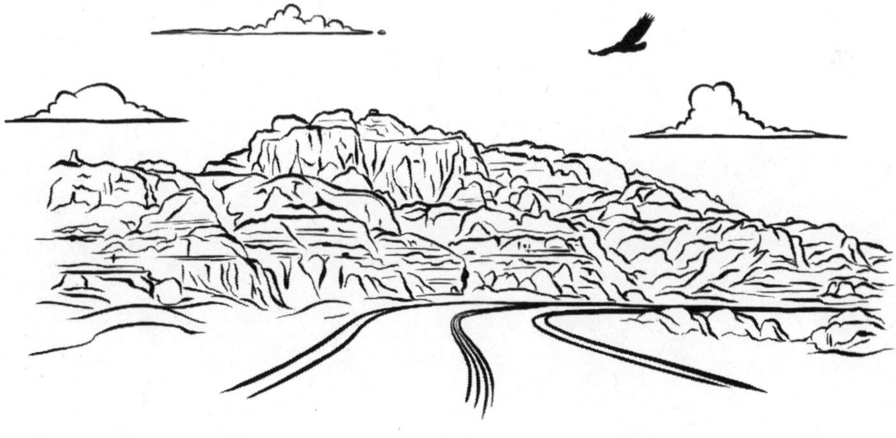

PT. 3

thiognak̄a wahi
mak̇a miksuye
wiċaḣp̄i ojíji t̄aŋyaŋ yahí
woablak̄ela iydwaye
maċaŋt̄e waṡt̄e.

RECONNECTING

I descend
from matriarchs,
from warriors,
from those who speak
the language of this land.

I arise
from the cracks of broken treaties,
from the fragments of unkept promises,
from the open wound of genocide.

I breathe
the prayers of *wiċahuŋk̄ak̄e*,
follow their guidance I find
in the sky,
on the land,
in the water,
in my dreams.

My *wiċahuŋk̄ak̄e* lived in a way
so that I may live as a bridge,
connecting their stories,
their language,
their power
to my children
and their children
and their children.

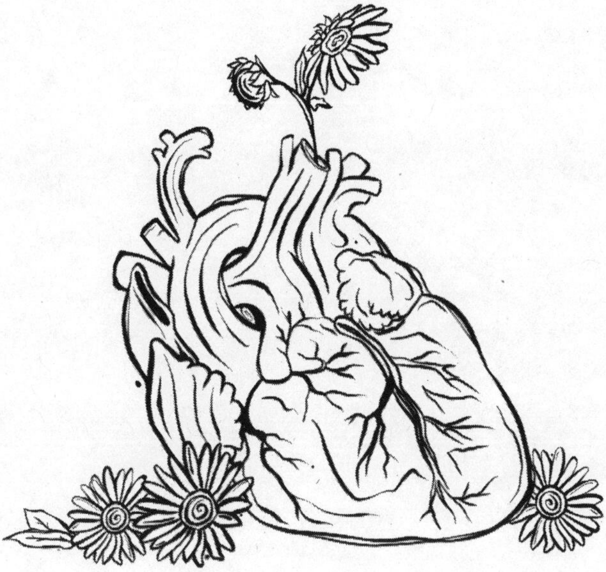

2.

NAĠI

(SOUL)

step one

I do not recognize my hands.

I look down
and I see the scars,
mostly from scabs I picked at
from scrapes received by
falling off my bicycle
racing up and down the backroads
of my childhood home
chasing ghosts.

These scars remind me
that these hands are mine.

But remembering is only step one
in the process of reconnecting the dots.

The process of reclaiming what was lost.

I do not recognize my face.

I look in the mirror
and I see what I believe is me,
but I'm quickly reminded that it is only a reflection.
A reflection of a person with pain buried so deep,
I'm scared to start diggin'
because I'm scared of what I'll find.
And if and when I find it,
I'm scared there'll be no way out,
no way back to the light.

But recognizing that there is pain there
in the first place, is step one
in the process of healing.

I do not recognize my body.

Nor do I give it much attention at all,
full of stretch marks,
mended bones,
aches and pains,
and mental lows.

At a young age,
I was taught that everything I am
is but a sacrifice to this world.
I was taught to work myself to the bone,
assimilate to the status quo.

I was taught that my body
is a doormat that says "welcome to our home"
because making others feel comfortable
as they stomp down on the parts of me
that bring them discomfort,
was my only means for my survival.

So I put in the hours,
and carried the weight of
disconnect with self
on my back
like a bad habit.

I carried it until I collapsed into depression,
and watched helplessly
as the world I was sold
crumbled on top of me.

I suffocated under the rubble until I realized
the only way to find breath again
was to pulled myself to the surface
and breathed in the fresh air
of a new beginning.

A new chance to connect those dots
that make an outline of self,
myself,
so I can fill in the spaces
of who I am,
who I truly am,
for the first time.

I do not fully recognize myself at this time.

But step one is the realization
that I am worth being seen.

the storms I've weathered

I remember the storms I've weathered
and fall in love with my strength
that carried me through.

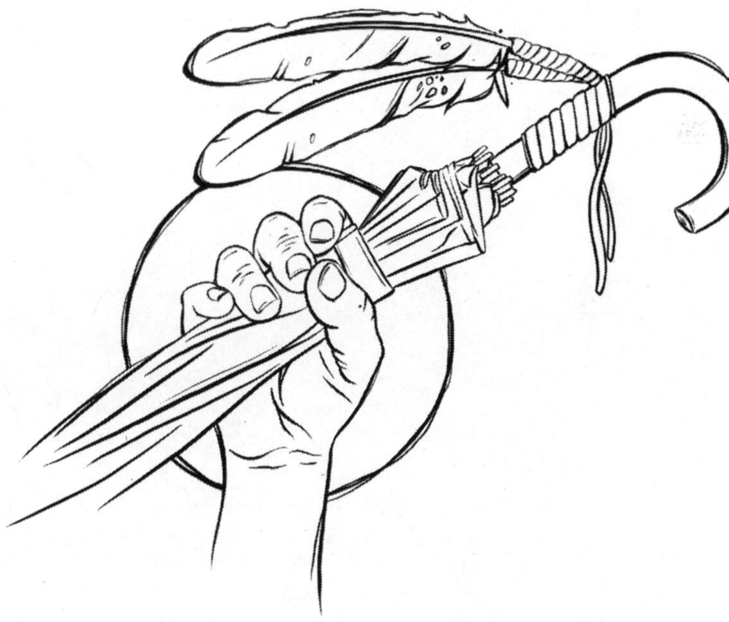

hiŋhaŋni waśte

The moon finds rest
as the sun whispers *hiŋhaŋni waśte.*

My bones
stiff from the gravity of life
loosen.

I throw my feet off the edge of the bed
and feel them land on the floor.

I breathe in,
breathe out.

I know some days will be rainy,
some full of clouds,
but I pray today is a day
I find a way
to fall a little bit more in love
with myself.

sacred flower

I am a glorious mess,
a collection of holy water
found inside a coffee-stained
styrofoam cup.

I am a beautiful mistake,
a rendition of Van Gogh
resurrected on whiteboard
during study hall,
accidentally done with
permanent marker.

I am a quiet shattering,
a soul falling from the sky
and crashing somewhere between
normalcy and insanity.

I am a sacred flower
shedding suffocating weeds,
slowly accepting everything I am
and letting go of everything else.

self-gratitude

I deserve
to touch my own skin
with gratitude,
feel my ribs and know
there is a beating heart underneath
that fills my veins like rivers
flowing to give me life.
My body carries me,
and I'm thankful it does
even on those days
I can hardly move,
because it's helped me get through,
helped me still be here.

finding myself

There are roads in my heart
waiting for me to travel them
on a late night drive,
kissing the white lines
with my headlights
as they take me places
not yet known.

This holy adventure
is where I find the pieces
of my being
that have been waiting patiently
for me to hit the open road
and find my way to them.

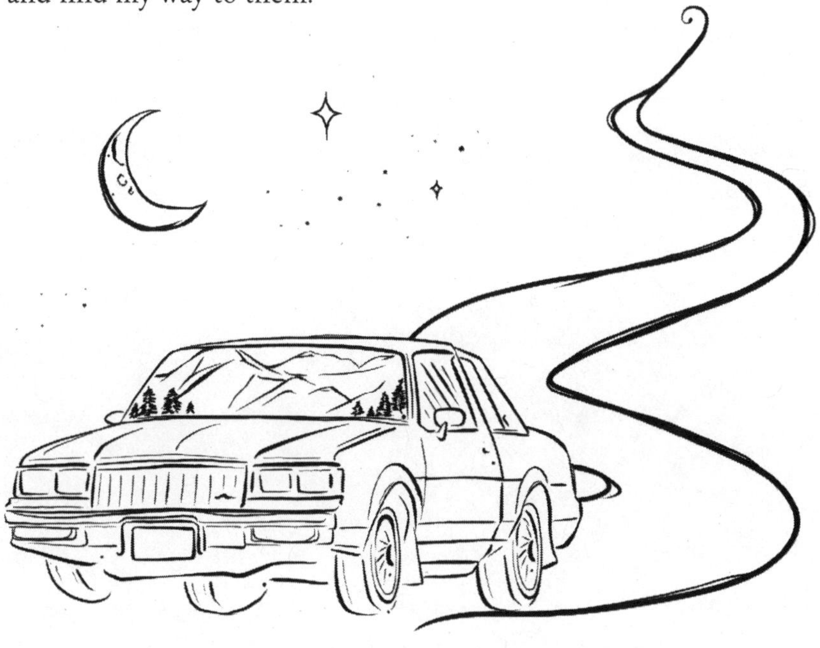

warmth

I am the fragments of a broken home
pieced together like patches
on a heavily worn hand-me-down.

I am a sweater full of holes.
But still, I can keep myself warm.

scrapes and cuts

The first thing I see
when I look at my hands
is the scars left behind
from scabs I wouldn't leave alone.

Scrapes and cuts
from afternoons riding my bike
down dirt roads.
Always a little too fast
because when you are young,
you always feel safe.

You always feel safe
because this world has yet to break you.

So I'd give myself up
as a sacrifice
to the momentum
of the hilly dirt roads
until I'd lose control
on a patch of loose dirt
and spill over my handlebars
in dramatic fashion.

Fresh wounds
tended to by grandma
with bandaids
that would never stay on,
exposing my scabs
for the world to see.

I'd find myself picking at them
because I never understood
that time was the healer
of wounds.

And as I ponder my impatience
that I've carried with me
well into adulthood,
I can't help but think
how my heart must look the same.

home sweet home

I'm falling in love
with the way
home sweet home
follows me
wherever I go.

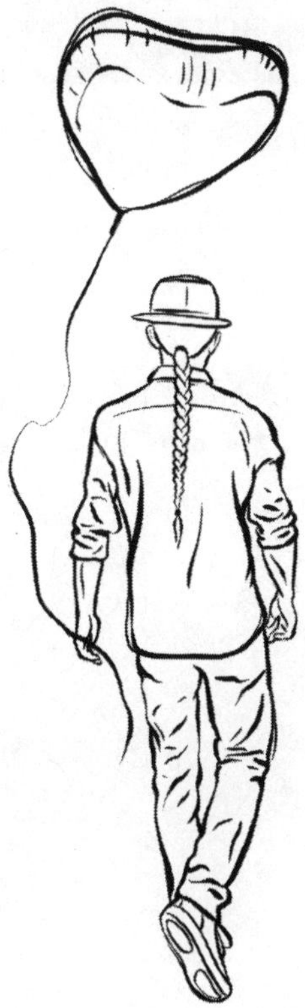

our bodies, warriors for our breath

My veins
flow courageously,
finding their way
to my heart
even on those days
I can't find a way
myself.

My lungs
inflate with tenacity,
gifting me with life
even on those days
meaning is hard
to find.

I find it beautiful
how our bodies
fight for our breathe
even on those days
we don't know
how much fight
we have left.

I will explode

I'm going to be me
so unapologetically,
my soul will explode
from the overwhelming healing
and joy
and the fragments will form
a galaxy in the sky.

garden chest

I found the strength to pry open my ribs
and till the soil within I've neglected for years,
reclaiming this abandoned lot of a chest
for a garden.

I'll plant all the beautiful things
right before I dance in the rain,
palms up to receive the love I've always deserved.

I'll dance in the rain
until the seeds buried deep in my bones
crack open and give birth
to the forest that lives in my soul.

This is where I find shelter.
This is where I find home.

the dust beneath my ribcage

found a heart / inside my chest / abandoned /
forgotten / left behind / still beating /
patiently waiting / for me to come back / and care for it / fully

storm chaser

I'm jealous of the rain
and the way it so freely
loses itself in the moment.

Raindrops kiss my cheek
as I look up at the clouds.
This is the only time
water slides down my face
without me apologizing
for being a burden.

I'm jealous of the lightning
and the way it so fiercely
pierces the sky.

The light flashes
as if to say,
"I am here. See me. Hear me"
and I can't help but think about
every damn time I felt shame
for wanting my voice to be heard.

I’m jealous of this thunderstorm,
and the way it so boldly
refuses to be still.

The clouds roll through
and I chase them
for just a taste of what it feels like
to be unapologetically free.

I am a poem

I am a poem,
like the flower that grows from the tree stump.

I am a poem,
like the broken-winged butterfly that still finds its way.

I am a poem,
like the peace found in hearing birds sing.

I am a poem,
every inch of my being.

I am a poem,
adding periods. where I. want to.

I am a poem,
putting line
breaks wherever I
choose.

I am a poem,
and so are you.

so
are
you.

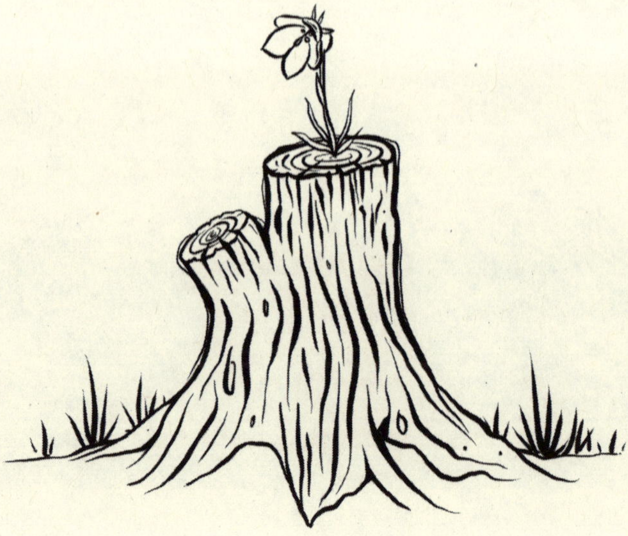

a note to my younger self

Thank you for carrying me to this moment
and never giving up on me.

crashing sound

I fell in love
with the crashing sound
of the walls falling down
that stood between me
and finding myself.

shards

I shatter,
pick up the pieces,
and start again.

Hands full of cuts
from handling
the parts of me
with sharp edges.

I am reminded
that growth
isn't always flower petals.

Sometimes,
it is shards of glass.

Sometimes,
it cuts deep
to the point
you want to run.

But I've learned to stay.

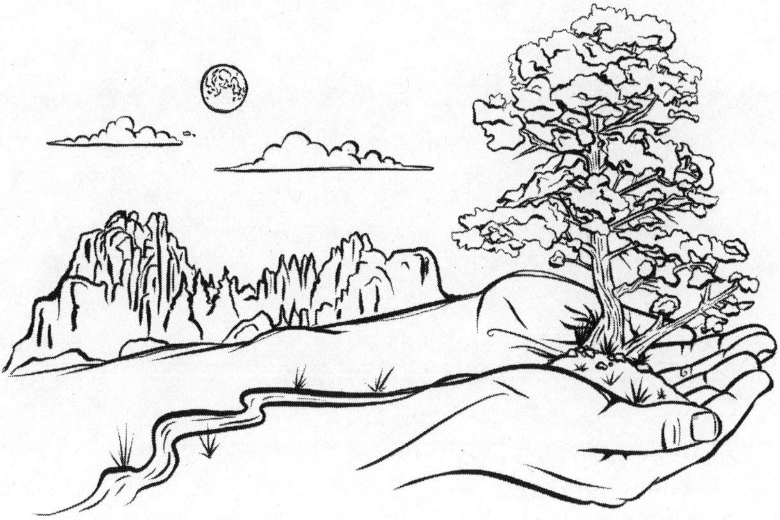

3.

UŊČI MAK̇A

(grandmother earth)

as the rain falls

The rain falls and lightly kisses my skin,
making me feel like I'm swimming in the ocean
as it bathes my soul in the vastness.

Yes, I still carry the brokenness of my being.

But I also feel oneness with the beauty
this earth shows me so selflessly.

So I'll just keep dancing in the rain,
like the petals and the leaves,
like a soul that is worthy.

pavement prayers

I went for a walk to either find home
or run from it.
It's hard to know where I'm going
when I'm still learning how to be here.

The uneven sidewalks tell me secrets,
told me there is a poem in the cracks
of the pavement.

So I fell to my knees
and touched each blade of grass
growing in the cracks
and until the words formed
and the lines fell in place.

This is what softening looks like,
the breaking of cement
with blades of grass.

This is what softening looks like,
a rewilding of what we were meant to be
before we paved over the gardens in our hearts.

I reached inside my rib cage
and found the same poem.

Dear River,

Make me smooth like the driftwood
and carry me with your soft hands
to all the places I once believed
I didn't deserve to take up space in.

Show me how to rest
in the current
and find life
on the shore of stillness.

Continue to teach me
as I close my eyes and lean into
the oneness of the movement and flow.

I thank you for holding me close
and revealing to me
the most important thing I now know,
which is how the capacity of joy grows
when we slowly let go of the fear of the unknowing
that rests beyond the river bend.

autumn leaves (lesson 1)

Are the first yellow leaves on the tree
the first to give up?

Or have they simply embraced letting go
to give space to grow something new?

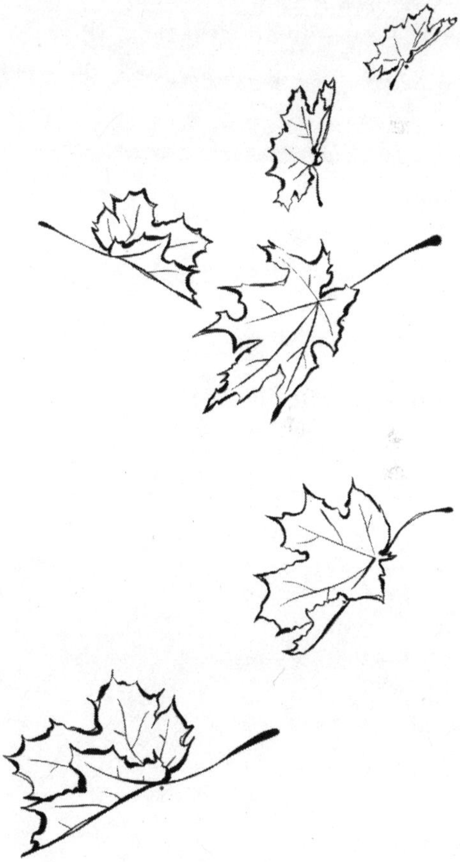

a story about gentleness and its ability to make a difference in this world

a single branch / a soft breeze / benevolent swaying /
the unforgiving heat from the sun / a plethora of leaves /
a soul finding rest beneath the tree

I now know what it means to be a feather in the wind

Wind,
what are you telling me
with the way you kiss my skin
so gently
yet so full of passion?

I wonder where I,
too,
can find such vigor
for simply being.

You touch my scars
without judgement
as if you've known me
forever.

And you do the same
to the trees,
the blades of grass,
and I can't help but sit in awe
as you dip your hands
in the Missouri River
and cause the ripples to dance
toward their own infinity.

I wonder if the way you kiss me
brings about the same ripples,
the same dance toward infinity,
within myself,
within my bones.

I just want to know
the secrets you hold.

So take me,
paint me with your breath,
and fill my lungs with your lessons.

I'll never stop listening to you,
oh wind,
the breath of *Uŋčí Makȟa*.

dandelions

Dandelions speckle my yard
and keep me company
with their bright yellow salute.

They remind me
of the new season
and shine like the sun
that kisses my skin.

I pick a ripe one,
and blow gently on it
until the seeds scatter.

They dance slowly to the ground,
and I think about my life.

I think about how
I want to live in a way
that shows my truest colors.
And as I age
and my hair turns white
just like these dandelions,
I want to leave behind the seeds
for a better tomorrow.

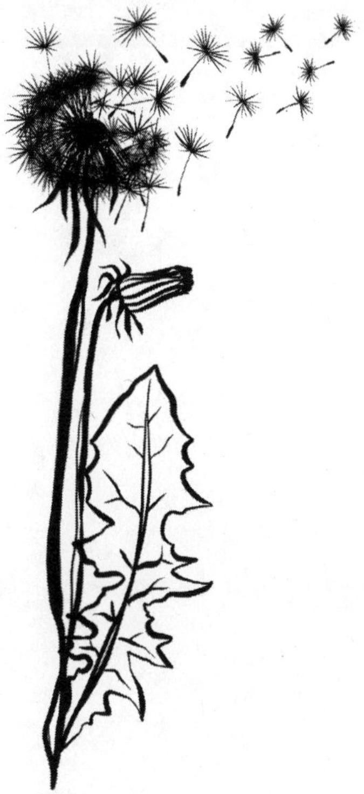

on a walk, I grew

The sun told me to slow down.

The sky taught me how to be still.

The trees beckoned me to look around.

The breeze showed me how to take it all in.

The flowers graced me with their beauty.

The memory of this moment fell into my pocket.

Uηc̄i Mak̇a whispered,

"Carry it with you. Never let it go."

like the rain

I am like the rain.
Even when I fall in the dirt,
I carve a path
and claim the space I deserve,
just like the rivers do.

skipping rock

I want to be like the skipping rock.

Toss me into the air
and let me taste the freedom of flight.

Let me kiss the *mniwaŋča* just enough
to hop back up for a short while
and watch closely
as the ones around me experience joy.

Celebrate, not mourn,
as I kiss the *mniwaŋča*
one last time and sink to the bottom.

Leave me there and let it be
my final resting place.

I don't want to be found and kept forever.
I want to be lost in the moment enough
to only be remembered.

the fireflies in the backyard

I beckoned a firefly to land on my hand.

And like I was existing a dream,
it touched my palm softly.

I begged for it to tell me its secrets.

I wanted to understand how it exists
unwavering
steadfast
as a dancing light
in the calm of night.

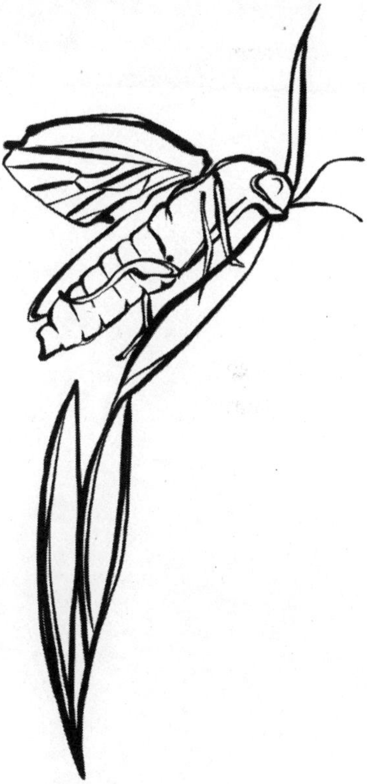

I waited a moment
and I swear I heard it say

"just know who you are."

In which I replied,

"what if I don't?"

As swiftly as this moment
became to be
it lifted from my hand
and decided to speak
one last time,

"start there."

mniwaŋc̄a sings

Mniwaŋc̄a sings
such glorious songs.
We learn the melody
only when
we are still long enough
to listen.

morning fog

The morning fog
dissipates into oblivion,
but I still carry with me
how I felt when
I danced in it.

autumn leaves (lesson 2)

Let the changing color of the leaves
teach us what revolution looks like.
Let it teach us how to shed the old
and grow something new.

front porch

I sat on the porch and closed my eyes.
I listened to the squirrels rustling
in the leaves.

The wind kissed my cheek
and I breathed softly.

I rocked back and forth in the chair
and found myself thinking about
our farmhouse living room
and the rocking chair my grandpa
would sit in.

The wind picked up
and the chill autumn breeze
gave me a shiver.

I opened my eyes to see the squirrels
chase one another through the leaves
and up the trees.

I thought to myself
there must be a poem here,
some divine lesson
I need to dissect out of it
and take for myself.

So I began trying to fit this moment
in a line
in a stanza
on a page
caged away.

It felt like I was trying to catch the leaves.
I could hold a few in my hands
but the rest beg to remain free.

So I gave this moment back to the wind,
watched it blow away into a swirl of memory
and I write these words to remind myself of the poetry
that already lives in the stillness.

holy ground

Even the dust has a place.
Where it goes and where it settles
is holy ground
if we believe that it is.
Everything is connected.
I am connected,
as I am now
and when I become dust.

the ways we speak

I speak to the juniper tree
with my hands
as I brush the branches
with my fingertips
in silence.

I speak to the *čeṫaŋ* above
with my gaze
breathing in
its wisdom and protection
in silence.

I find space to grow
in the silence.

It's in the silence
I find the wisdom
for when I should speak
with words.

river stone

I am a stone in a river,
solid in my being
while the water
washing over me,
slowly smoothing
my sharp edges.

I call this a softening.

I call this becoming.

what the trees can teach us

We do not ask the trees
to grow different leaves.

Or tell them when it's time to
shed their leaves and rest.

Or question the validity of their roots
and the way they grow, unseen.

What we witness
as we stand beneath
their towering branches,
what we feel
when we brush against
their bark with our fingertips
is their beauty of being
just as they are now
and their becoming
according to their own timing.

sequoia seeds

Sequoia seeds
split open
crack open
and give birth to a life
prayed into existence
by *Uŋčī*.

In these same moments
this seedling
stretches its roots
to take hold of
its relatives' roots,
and here I am taught
what it means to be
interwoven with
community.

A forest can only grow
when we are connected with
all our relatives.

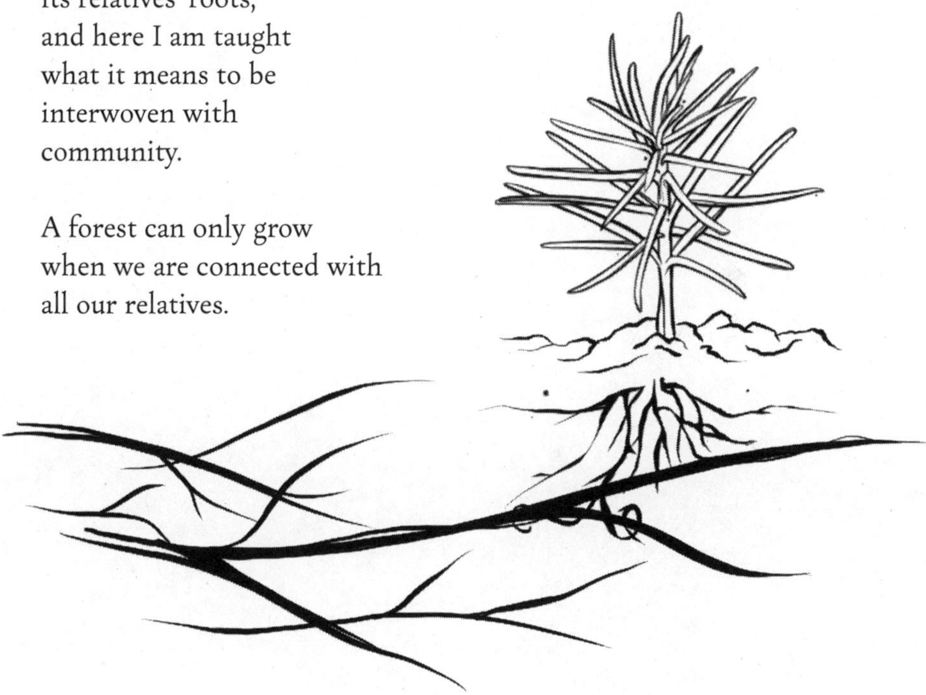

I am

I am nature, growing roots.
I am nature.
I am   growing.
I am   roots.
I am.

barefoot

I am most at peace
barefoot in the grass,
becoming one with the roots
that understand better than I do
how lucky we are
to call *Uŋčí Makȟa*
home.

enough

I went for a walk in the rain
to wash myself clean
from every part of me
I do not like.

As my clothes became wet,
became heavy,
I looked down at my hands
to see water drip from the edge of my sweater.

I thought to myself
"I am just like the clouds."
So I put my hands out
and watched as the raindrops
fell from every inch of my body.

This wasn't a cleansing.
Rather, it was a shared release of the weight
that exists so inherently on *Uŋči Maḣa*
and in us all.

I, for so long, have carried this shame
given to me from past trauma
hoping something someday
would wash me clean from it.

But the clouds reminded me
that I am already enough
to grow,
to become,
to be set free.

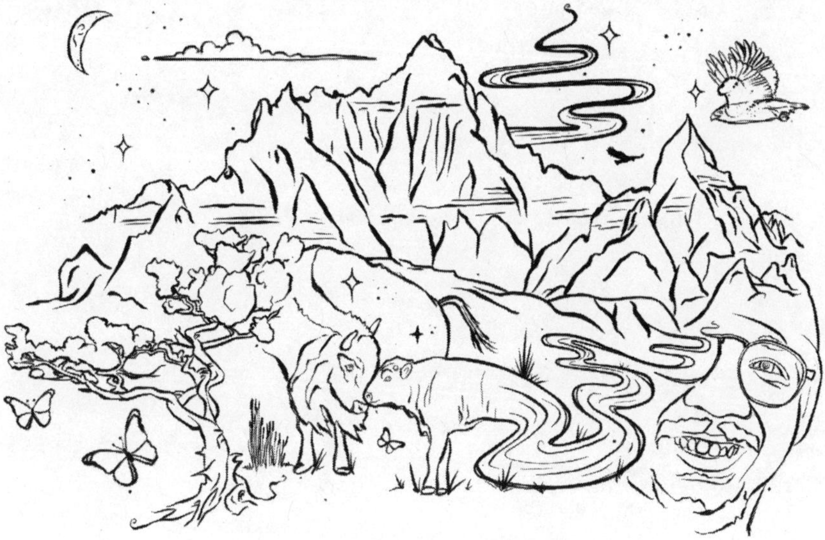

4.

MIT̄AK̄UYEP̄I

(my relatives)

as the fence lines are swallowed whole

I think about how those who came
nearly wiped out the *tata̅ŋka*,
their continued existence on *Oċeti Ṡa̅kowiŋ* land
speaks of resilience.

Resilience is a word that sits heavy with me.
It tells a story that wrong has been done.

I think about my *wiċahuŋ̅ka̅ke*
and what they endured for me to be here.

I'm thankful for their resilience,
still here despite the wrongs that have been done.
Broken treaties.
Broken promises.
Broken relationship with the land,
exploited by those who only wanted to capitalize.

As I travel out west,
I look out my car window
and watch the fences that line the roads slice by
like small cuts.

What a construct,
this idea that we must draw lines in the dirt
to make a here and a there.

But I see resilience,
the hills and mountains and the plants that find home
on the shifting landscapes.
Like the desert spoon
that poked my finger,
reminding me I'm simply a visitor here
so I made it an offering
to give thanks for its lesson.

We are all visitors,
sharing space for only a season.
Our bodies offering a quick breath
before we find ourselves on our journey beyond.

What this future hold
I do not know,
but in the end,
I believe every fence line will be swallowed whole
by the soil
and we will roam free like the *tataŋka*.

No longer living inside ghostly lines,
no more a here and there.
Just here
present with *Uŋci Maka*
and every relative who shares space with her.

So while I am here,
daily I ask myself
what I will breathe life into
and help grow
with this one quick breath
I hold.

the day after (the 4th)

After the smoke settles,
the true fireworks remain:

the lightning on the horizon,
the dancin' fireflies,
the stars in the sky,
my favorite finale, *haŋwi*,
and the fire inside of us all
that lights our hope
we carry today
for a better tomorrow.

still hope

The creek ignites with fireworks,
quietly.

What a miracle it is
to see the sky reach down
and touch the water
with such soft hands.

Birds sing in the distance
as the gentle rolling hills
beckon me to get lost over their horizon.

Construction saws slice through this holy moment
to build a single family home across the creek.

A train rumbles through
and shakes the earth to its bones.

The water tells me it's sick by its color,
as it's forced to carry pollutants from upstream.

But the creek still ignites in celebration,
as the raindrops explode on its surface to acknowledge its
survival.

Acknowledging how it is,
although scarred and in pain,
still here since the war that started against it in 1492.

A little baby fish swims up to the rock I'm sitting on and tells
me,

"Keep fighting, there is still hope."

weapons of war

I see a trailer with an excavator
heading north
and I wonder what it's destination will be
because I see a weapon
ready to wage war on *Uŋčī Mak̇a*.

Cut open to exploit,
to leave scars
that our children
and our children's children
will feel.

I feel sorrow,
a deep ache in my soul
and I pray for the day
we no longer have to talk about
how resilient *Uŋčī Mak̇a* is,
because I envision a day
where she is healed
and we are living in oneness
with her
once more.

celebrate Indigenous joy

Indigenous laughter is radical joy
in the flesh.
Every cackle that resurrects
from our bellies
is like a ghost
that haunts these lands'
so-called forefathers.

I'm learning to celebrate
our Indigenous happiness
just as much as I celebrate
our Indigenous perseverance.

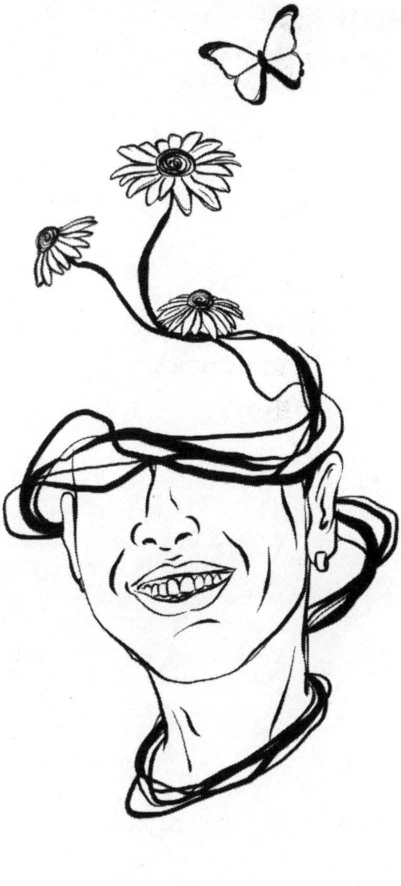

occupied land

Ownership is a construct,
weaponized jargon we drown in
while picking up the pieces of violence.

Colonizers came
in not a good way
and what we have to show
for their bitter fruit
are fences
and wounds
that still bleed today.

This land is occupied,
not owned.

These fences,
petty lines drawn in the sand
are markings of a failing system,
a violent game the colonizer
will always lose.

This I know because
when we die
Uŋčī Maka swallows us whole
and turns us back into dirt.

She teaches us we are a part of her,
a small piece
of the circle of things
that make up her body.

And like the body,
the hand does not have authority
over the heart
or the head,
every piece has a place
and just is.

It is the fool
who believes otherwise.

a painting, slowly fading

What is the blue sky
if only viewed by our tired eyes
between the metal bars
erected by the "american dream"
as we carry the weight of a 9-5
that doesn't pay the rent,
barely puts food on the table?

A painting,
slowly fading in the distance
as we stare out the window of our jobs,
lining the pockets of a few
with silver and gold
as we grow old and weary,
just trying to catch a break.

But remember when they told us
to pull ourselves up by our bootstraps?
Well, when we did
they ripped
as if they weren't meant to withstand
in the first place.

The blue sky keeps fading
as we look between the bars that keep us caged.

And we drive home,
sometimes after the sun has set,
the blue sky is asleep
because unlike us
she is allowed to rest.

We chase the clouds, the mountains, the streams
as we cling to the scraps of the "american dream",
hoping to catch a glimpse of *Uŋc̄i Mak̇a* and her beauty
between the bars of this cage called freedom.

This is why I allow myself to dream beyond
the fading painting of the blue sky,
beyond these bars that keep us caged,
and fight so that one day we can touch the sky ourselves
as we fly around the mountains and over the streams
like the *ċet̄aŋ*,
like the *waŋbli*,
exist in the midst of it all
exactly in the way our souls were meant to.

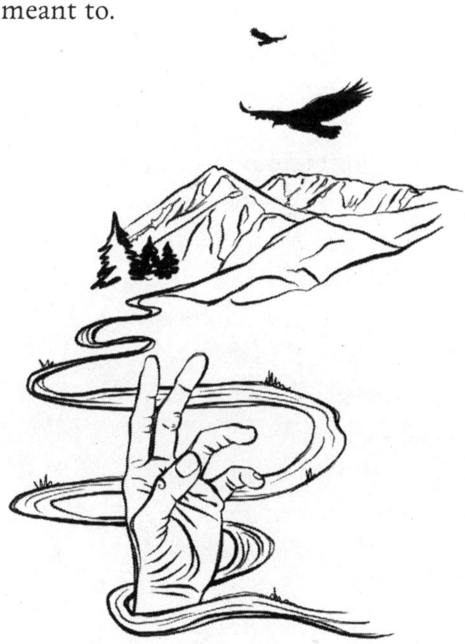

roots

Wagon wheel wounds run deep,
but my roots in *Ḣe Sap̄a* run deeper
hold stronger
keep me grounded.

I read stories of resistance,
from my Laḱot̄a ancestors
to the Black Panthers.

I realize the "american dream"
is just american dread,
and my heart aches
for every single one of us colonized
by those who represent the flag
I was forced to pledge allegiance to
as an elementary school kid.

But I remember these stories of resistance.
I hear in the distance my ancestors
fighting to protect *Oċeti Ṡak̄owiŋ*
and I joyfully inherit the fight
against every colonial state
across *Uŋc̄i Maḱa*
that is built to oppress.

I stand against every bullet that flies from the oppressor.

I stand with every bullet that flies from the oppressed.

I stand until we all are free.

murmurs of change

I hear murmurs of change
in between the sounds of news stories.
Another person froze to death.
Another person shot by those who are supposed to protect.
Another girl missing.
Just more of the same.

I hear murmurs of change,
was handed a seed
and was told to be patient,
it takes time to grow.

So I planted it in the ground I was sold
by the "american dream".
Followed the rules,
watered it with my vote
and my words
and my actions
hoping these murmurs of change
would come.

But the seed would not sprout
started to voice my frustrations out loud.
"Change comes slowly" I was told,
gaslit to believe the lies I was sold.

I hear murmurs of change,
but nothing comes of it
and I'm starting to wonder
if these murmurs are only meant
to keep us still.

I wonder what has poisoned the soil,
and who benefits from keeping the seeds of change
stagnant.

Once we find who fears the gardens of the people
from rising up
and sprouting into a beautiful new world,
that is where we must begin,
that is where we can rid the soil of contaminates
and grow a revolution.

radical community

Show up for your kin.
Stay there.
Be there always.
Embody the collective struggle.
Learn in community.
Grow in community.
Let our discomfort teach us
as we listen about experiences
that aren't our own.
Celebrate joy together.
Hold space for grief together.
Fight.
Fight.
Never stop fighting
until we find
liberation for all.

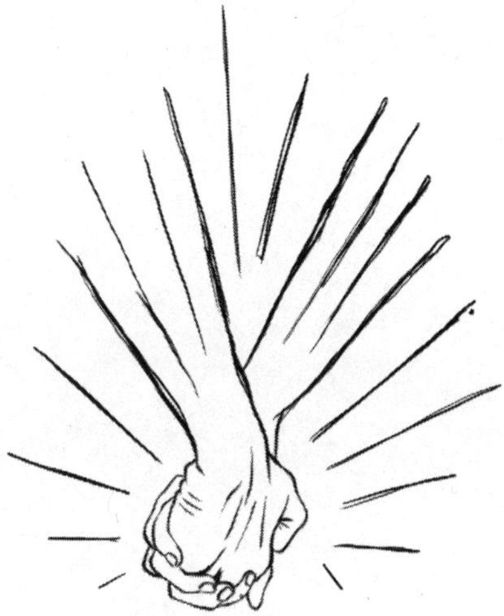

when healing comes

Every place
the grass touches
the sun kisses
the roots run through
the waters quench
the mountains rest on
the sand sits
is land
that was never meant
to be owned.

Borders only exist
to oppress.

In the end
all fences
all walls
will fall.

together

Sometimes my heart beats
and sometimes it bleeds.

When it does,
I turn to the stars
and they offer the crescent moon
as a tourniquet
and I find peace.

Sometimes the stillness
wraps its arms around me
and sometimes the silence
is deafening.

When it comes,
I turn to the wind
and they offer me their song
through the rustling prairie grass
and I find peace.

Sometimes my feet
carry me through,
and sometimes the weight of it all
brings me to my knees.

When it does,
I turn to the collective,
the warriors of all that is good
and they remind me
just how much power we carry
when we stack all our bones
together in resistance
to what crushes us,
together to build a world
that remembers that this land,
the stars,
and all that live and grow here,
are our relatives.

And I find peace.

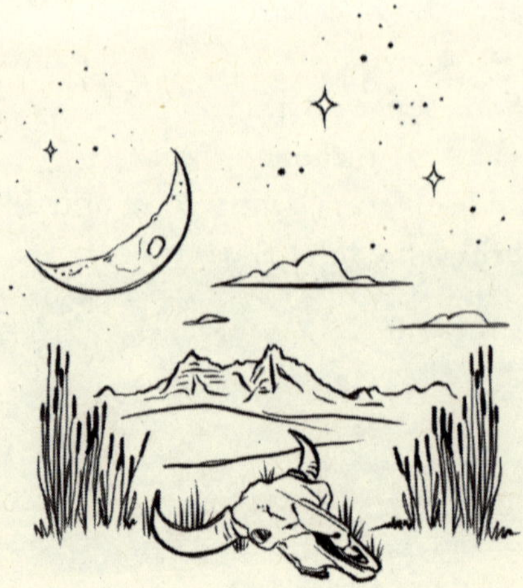

GLOSSARY

ċet̄aŋ - hawk
haŋwi - moon
hiŋhaŋni waśt̄e - good morning
Ḣe Sap̄a - Black Hills
hokśic̄ala - baby
mak̇a - dirt
Mit̄ak̄uyep̄i - my relatives
mni - water
Mniluzahaŋ - Rapid Creek, Rapid City
mniwaŋc̄a - ocean
naği - soul
Oċeti Ṡak̄owiŋ - The Seven Council Fires
Ak̄iċit̄a - warrior
ṫataŋk̄a - buffalo
Uŋc̄i - grandmother
Uŋc̄i Mak̇a - grandmother earth
wak̄iŋyaŋ - thunder-beings
wanaği - start spirit, spirit
waŋbli - eagle
wi - sun
wiċahuŋk̄ak̄e - ancestors
wowaś'ak̄e - strength

thiognak̄a wahi - I have come home
mak̇a miksuye - the earth remembers me
wiċaḣp̄i ojiji t̄aŋyaŋ yahi - the stars whisper "it is good that you came"
woablak̄ela iyewaye - I find calm
maċaŋt̄e waśt̄e - My heart is good

ABOUT

Robert Harold Bordeaux

poet

Robert Harold Bordeaux is a Sičaŋǧu Lakȟóta descendant and a writer and activist whose community is the Rosebud Reservation. He was raised by his grandparents in the small community of Erwin, South Dakota. Growing up disconnected from his Lakȟóta roots, his life has been a journey to find his way home to the Rosebud Reservation to share space and grow in relationship with his tiwahe (family). In his writing, he touches on this journey connecting with his Lakȟóta roots as he learns from Uŋči Makȟa what it means to be a good relative and ancestor. He shares openly about his life through his books, content shared online, and speaking. Outside of writing, Bordeaux is active in carrying on his ancestors' legacy of fighting for sovereignty through his activism around abolition of colonial systems.

His previous work includes his debut poetry collection *Lovely Seeds* (2017), *Quiet Remnants* (2018), a short story in the anthology *Disconnected* (2018), and various poems found in previous editions of South Dakota Poetry Society's literary magazine *Pasque Petals*.

Thomasina Topbear

artist

Thomasina TopBear is a self taught artist from the Oglala Lakȟóta & Santee Dakota Nations. She is a member of the international all female paint crew Few & Far Women and co-founded City Mischief Murals. Specializing in large-scale murals her work can be seen on the sides of buildings throughout the country. Thomasina has organized a number of events focusing on empowering and creating safe spaces for youth and fellow artists to practice their crafts. She draws her influences from her Očeti Šakȟowiŋ culture while using art to express her thoughts on community, social justice, spirituality and togetherness.